To Alta....

my dear friend
and buddy....
Thank you for your
purchase...

Love Cheryl
Brandon
8/23/09

Thoughts of Wisdom

Cheryl Brandon

authorHOUSE®

AuthorHouse™
1663 Liberty Drive
Bloomington, IN 47403
www.authorhouse.com
Phone: 1-800-839-8640

First published by AuthorHouse 8/5/2009

ISBN: 978-1-4389-8454-4 (sc)

Library of Congress Control Number: 2009904669

Printed in the United States of America
Bloomington, Indiana

This book is printed on acid-free paper.

Contents

Acknowledgements

THANKS TO: First I want to thank God for giving me the gift of poetry

AUTHORHOUSE PUBLISHING for getting my work out!

HARLEMPRIDE REC/ REV ISLAM

UNITEHERE L-100 for giving me a vehicle to utilize my writing @ Strikes and Rallies!!

TERRI B. MILLS for spreading my thoughts of wisdom to others.

WE PRINT T- SHIRTS / PAPA DURIF

T- SHIRT SALES TEAM/ LORENZO DAVIDS, SHARON ESWICK, RHONDA JACKSON

MAC HARLEM/ MAC ARTIST/ BETHANY ELKIN

Dedications

FRANK AND SANDRA BRANDON

DELORES BOYD, Who pushed me constantly to expose my quotes to the world.

Introduction

This book is for those who appreciate the gift of thought. I was inspired to write my thoughts because of my life experiences, also because of things I've witnessed in life that encouraged me to form an opinion.

As you read through the thoughts of wisdom quotes, you may find comments at the end to help you understand why I wrote it. I hope you enjoy reading this book, as it is guaranteed to give you something to think about.

The poems I've written were inspired by love, life and labor. However, sometimes a poem becomes a song and life should be something to write about.

Cheryl Brandon

Bio Poem

This is my autobiography
Put this poem in the rap category
I want the fame and the glory
I'm from the west side with a story
I'm about to reminisce
First things first, born January 26
God created a poet, so here's my poetry
I have to give some praise because he blessed me
So we all should say our prayers
I know I'm glad that he brought me here
The next praise goes to my Mom and Dad
I used to be mad he was strict but now I'm glad
And, the apple don't fall far from the tree
Because my father loved music that inspired me
Since I was 10 years old, these stories never told
Because of my mother intellect, I stayed on the honor roll
I kept a 95, sometimes a 99
My father once asked the teacher was he out his mind
Yeah I press rewind, let me go back in time
They used to call me Cher Rock, I wrote my first rhyme
Talent was discovered, only put God above it
I stepped up to the mic and the people loved it
Yeah it's something there, it's something in the air
I got my pen and my pad and started heading here
So here I am, and here's my story
I didn't get the fame yet, but I got the glory
And my sister and brothers all could testify
It's not what we had it's what we have inside
And were alright and were all tight
We love each other and guess what, we all write.
My brother loves his denim, my sister's Ms. fashion vision
My brother got the makings of a Quincy Jones in him
Terri gives her 2 cents Shaun is stingy
Rev expensive lifestyle inspires me
Conceited nah, but we all know who we are

My gift of poetry made me Cheryl Starr
So here I go again back with this pad and pen
I write deep poetry so read this to the end
And on that note, let me clear my throat
It's thoughts of wisdom because it's wisdom in the thoughts I wrote

This is me at 10 years old

My parents sitting from left to right my Bro's & Sis, that's me in middle

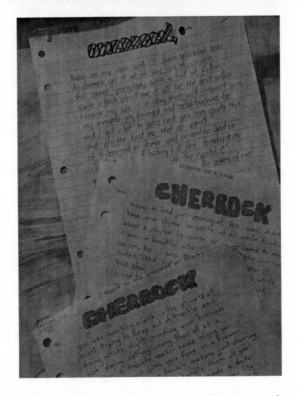

The archives –those are my poems I wrote when I was about 15 years old. I was Cher Rock then.

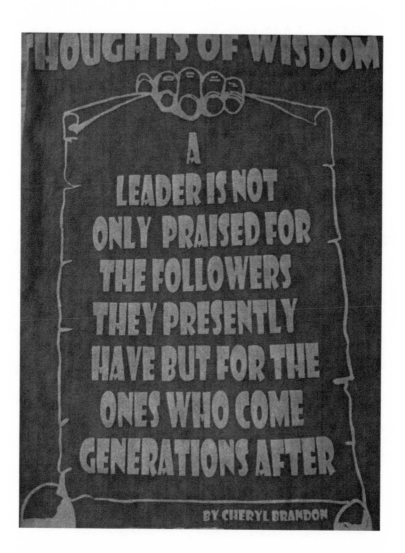

Thoughts Of Wisdom:

A TEACHER IS NOT ONLY SOMEONE WHO GUIDES YOU THROUGH A LESSON, BUT SOMEONE WHO STEPS BACK SO YOU CAN LEARN ONE.

SOMETIMES WE HAVE TO TEACH THROUGH SILENCE BECAUSE SILENCE IS OFTEN LOUDER THAN WORDS.

Thoughts Of Wisdom:

PEOPLE WITH TALENT HAVE THE ABILITY TO LEARN BUT PEOPLE WITH SKILLS HAVE THE ABILITY TO TEACH

Thoughts Of Wisdom:

THE PURSUIT OF ANYTHING IS WHATEVER GOAL YOU SET TO GET IT, THE REWARD OF EVERYTHING IS WHATEVER GOAL YOU'VE COMPLETED

THEIRS NOTHING LIKE THE FINISH LINE

Thoughts Of Wisdom:

GOD ANSWERS PRAYERS AND HAS THE POWER TO CHANGE PEOPLE, SO HAVE YOU ASKED GOD TO SHOW YOU SOME CHANGES IN SOMEONE YOU'VE PRAYED ABOUT?

Thoughts Of Wisdom:

THE BEAUTY OF ART IS WHAT YOU PICTURE IT TO BE.
THE BEAUTY OF A PICTURE IS HOW YOU SEE IT.

ART IS UNEXPLAINABLE. IT'S ALL IN ONES OWN
IMAGINATION, THAT'S THE BEAUTY OF IT. THEY SAY
BEAUTY IS IN THE EYES OF THE BEHOLDER SO WE ALL
CAN SEE BEAUTY IN OUR OWN IMAGE.

Something To Think About:

YOU CAN CHANGE THE CHANNELS IN YOUR LIFE JUST
LIKE THE TELEVISION, BUT WHAT CAN YOU CHANGE
WHEN THE TELEVISION'S WATCHING YOU?

I WROTE THIS AT A TIME WHEN CELEBRITIES WERE
ALAWYS IN NEWS OR ON TELEVISION FOR SOMETHING
NEGATIVE

Thoughts Of Wisdom:

A LEADER IS NOT ONLY PRAISED FOR THE FOLLOWERS
THEY PRESENTLY HAVE, BUT FOR THE ONES WHO COME
GENERATIONS AFTER.

THOUGHT OF MARTIN LUTHER KING AND HIS
LEADERSHIP THEN AND NOW WE CONTINUE TO FOLLOW
HIS DREAM WITH PRESIDENT ELECT BARACK OBAMA.

Thoughts Of Wisdom:

LIFE IS ABOUT LEARNING LESSONS, EXPERIENCE IS ABOUT
TEACHING THEM, AND TEACHING THEM IS ABOUT
SPREADING THE WORD.

Thoughts Of Wisdom:

OPPORTUNITIES ARE LIKE SECONDS, THEY COME AND THEY GO AND IF YOU'RE NOT FAST ENOUGH, YOU'LL MISS YOURS.

ALWAYS BE PREPARED TO RECEIVE THE MANY OPPORTUNITIES LIFE MAY BRING, ESPECIALLY IF YOU'VE BEEN WAITING ON ONE.

Thoughts Of Wisdom:

PEOPLE WITH IDEAS USUALLY THINKS ABOUT MAKING THINGS HAPPEN, BUT PEOPLE WITH KNOWLEDGE GETS THINGS DONE.

Thoughts Of Wisdom:

THE TEXTURE OF SOMETHING USUALLY REPRESENTS ITS DURABILITY, SO TO HANDLE OBSTACLES IN LIFE YOU MUST HAVE THICK SKIN.

LIFE WILL PRESENT SOME REAL CHALLENGES FROM TIME TO TIME BUT SOMETIMES IT'S HOW WE HANDLE CHALLENGES THAT MAKES US STRONG.

Thoughts Of Wisdom:

A VICTORY IS SWEET WHEN YOUR CHALLENGED TO THE VERY END AND YOU WIN, AS OPPOSED TO SOMEONE WHO GIVES UP AND YOU WIN BECAUSE YOU WEREN'T CHALLENGED.

Thoughts Of Wisdom:

IT IS EASIER TO MAKE THE SAME MISTAKE TWICE,
THAN TO LISTEN ONCE

PEOPLE HAVE A HARD TIME LISTENING, AND MOST OF US
HAVE MADE NUMEROUS MISTAKES BECAUSE WE CHOSE
NOT TO TAKE ADVICE

Something To Think About:

DO WE IGNORE THE TRUTH ABOUT SOMEONE WE LOVE,
OR DO WE IGNORE SOMEONE WE LOVE ONCE WE KNOW
THE TRUTH ABOUT THEM?

Thoughts Of Wisdom:

A PERSON IS NOT TRULY CHANGED, UNTIL THEY CAN HELP CHANGE SOMEONE WHO IS EXACTLY LIKE THEY USE TO BE.

NOONE CAN TRULY UNDERSTAND SOMEONE UNLESS THEY HAVE WALKED IN THEIR SHOES AND IF THEY CAN GUIDE SOMEONE IN A BETTER DIRECTION THEY ARE EXAMPLES OF CHANGE.

Thoughts Of Wisdom:

YOU DONT HAVE TO GET ON A PLANE TO SEE THE WORLD, IT'S THE JOURNEYS YOU GO THROUGH IN LIFE THAT HELPS YOU SEE IT BETTER.

Something To Think About:

YOU DONT HAVE TO PARTY ALL YOUR LIFE,
TO BE THE LIFE OF THE PARTY

Something To Think About:

ARE PEOPLE AFRAID OF LEARNING, BECAUSE IT WOULD
CHALLENGE THEM TO TEACH?

Something To Think About:

WHY IS THERE SO MUCH RACISM IN THE WORLD, WHEN EVERYONE'S IN THE DARK UNTIL THINGS ARE BROUGHT TO LIGHT?

GOVERNOR SPLITZER SCANDAL

Something To Think About:

WHY ARE PEOPLE SO QUICK TO PASS JUDGEMENT ON OTHERS? IS IT BECAUSE SOMEONE THOUGHT THE WORSE OF THEM?

GIVE PEOPLE A CHANCE BEFORE YOU ASSUME THE WORSE AND MAYBE ONE DAY YOU WON'T HAVE TO PROVE YOURSELF TO SOMEONE WHO MISJUDGED YOU

Thoughts Of Wisdom:

BRILLIANCE ISN'T ONLY ABOUT YOUR SMARTS AND YOUR INTELLIGENCE, BUT BRILLIANCE IS IN THE ONE WHO DISCOVERED YOU.

THOUGHT OF AND DEDICATED TO OPRAH WINFREY BECAUSE SHE WAS THE FIRST PERSON I HEARD MENTION BARACK OBAMA'S BRILLIANCE.

Thoughts Of Wisdom:

IT'S NEVER TOO LATE TO SEEK KNOWLEDGE, AS LONG AS WHEN YOU RECEIVE IT, YOU SEEK TO UNDERSTAND IT

Thoughts Of Wisdom:

LOVE IS THE GREATEST GIFT GOD'S GIVEN US, AND THE GREATEST GIFT WE CAN GIVE SOMEONE WE LOVE, IS TO LOVE GOD THE GREATEST.

NOONE CAN DENY LOVING SOMEONE AND HAVING SOMEONE WHO LOVES YOU IS A BLESSING. I THANK GOD WHEN I COUNT MY BLESSINGS.

Something To Think About:

WHEN DO WE BELIEVE IN THE AMERICAN DREAM? , WHEN WE SEE PEOPLE FROM AMERICA LIVING THEIR DREAMS? , OR WHEN WE SEE DREAMS COME TRUE FOR THE AMERICAN PEOPLE? .

I BELIEVE, YES WE CAN, BARACK MADE AMERICAN PEOPLE BELIEVE IN AMERICA AGAIN.

Thoughts Of Wisdom:

DO WHAT YOU THINK ABOUT OR THINK ABOUT CHANGING YOUR THOUGHTS

Thoughts Of Wisdom:

IF YOU WANNA FIND YOUR FAWLS, LOOK AT YOUR CHILDREN IF YOU NEED TO FIND FAULT, LOOK AT YOUR PARENTS AND IF YOU NEED TO FIND GOD, THEN LOOK AT YOURSELF.

Thoughts Of Wisdom:

SOMETIMES GIVING SOMEONE DIRECTIONS IS MORE THAN HELPING THEM FIND A LOCATION, BUT PROVIDING A PATH FOR SOMEONE TO GO RIGHT INSTEAD OF LEFT

Something To Think About:

IN A WORLD OF RACISM, IS IT STILL IMPORTANT TO BE THE FIRST ONE TO GET A SEAT OR THE LAST ONE STANDING

THOUGHT OF THIS QUOTE WHEN SEAN BELL WAS SHOT.

Thoughts Of Wisdom:

FAME IS CONSIDERED BEING IN THE SPOTLIGHT SO
IF THE CAMERAS TURN ON YOU WHAT WILL YOU BE
FAMOUS FOR?

Something To Think About:

IF YOU THINK SMALL YOU WILL NEVER HAVE BIG IDEAS.

Thoughts Of Wisdom:

A SPEAKER IS ONLY POWERFUL IF SOMEONE'S LISTENING.

Something To Think About:

IS SUCCESS MEASURED BY WHAT OTHERS SEE OF US OR BY WHAT WE SEE OF OURSELVES?

Thoughts Of Wisdom:

PEOPLE CRY WHEN THEIR HAPPY, PEOPLE CRY WHEN THEIR SAD, THE DIFFERENCE IS THEIR REACTION WHILE CRYING.

Something To Think About:

YOU ARE WHO YOU ARE, AND WHO YOU ARE MAKES YOU, YOU.

Thoughts Of Wisdom:

GOD LOVES YOU, THAT'S WHY HE'S WORKING ON ME

Something To Think About:

BE THE ONE WHO STANDS OUT, THEN YOU'LL ALWAYS BE OUTSTANDING.

Thoughts Of Wisdom:

A SPEECH IS NOT ABOUT WHAT'S BEING SAID, BUT WHAT
THE PEOPLE WHO WERE THERE REMEMBERS

I WAS INSPIRED TO WRITE THIS QUOTE ONCE I SAW THE
GREAT DEBATERS

Thoughts Of Wisdom:

THE TRUTH HURTS, BUT SO DOES A LIE, ESPECIALLY IF
YOU'RE THE ONE BEING LIED TOO, SO I'D RATHER HURT
YOU WITH THE TRUTH

Something To Think About:

WHEN COPS ARE AROUND DO YOU FEEL SAFE? , OR DO YOU FEAR FOR YOUR LIVES?

Something To Think About:

IN A CANDIATE RACE, SHOULD RACE MATTER IN A CANDIATE?

WROTE THIS QUOTE WHEN OBAMA WON IOWA

Thoughts Of Wisdom:

IF WE KNEW ALL THE INGREDIENTS THAT GOES INTO A BOMB WE WOULD THINK TWICE THE NEXT TIME WE EXPLODE ON SOMEONE.

THIS QUOTE CAME TO ME AS I WATCHED MOVIE, THE KINGDOM

Thoughts Of Wisdom:

WHEN IT RAINS IT POURS, SO IF YOU NEED TO POUR OUT YOUR HEART TO SOMEONE, DO IT SO YOU CAN STOP CRYING

Thoughts Of Wisdom:

SOMEONE DOESN'T HAVE TO BE MADE OF GLASS FOR YOU TO SEE RIGHT THROUGH THEM

Thoughts Of Wisdom:

YOU DON'T HAVE TO QUOTE FAMOUS PEOPLE LINES TO BE HEARD, JUST TRY MAKING YOUR LINES FAMOUS

Something To Think About:

ARE PEOPLE AFRAID OF CHANGING BECAUSE IT WOULD TAKE AWAY THEIR EXCUSE TO ACT IGNORANT?

Something To Think About:

HUMILIATION IS WORSE THAN EMBRASSAMENT SO YOU SHOULD BE EMBRASSED IF YOU EVER HUMILIATED SOMEONE

Thoughts Of Wisdom:

HOPE IS WHAT SOMEONE WISHES FOR, FAITH IS WHAT SOMEONE PRAYS FOR, AND RELIGION IS WHAT SOMEONE STANDS FOR

Thoughts Of Wisdom:

A SPEAKER IS ONLY POWERFUL IF SOMEONE'S LISTENING, IS ANYONE LISTENING TO YOU?.

Something To Think About:

FOR BETTER OR WORSE, DOES THAT MEAN YOU LOVE SOMEONE FOR THE BETTER EVEN IF YOU SEE THE WORSE IN THEM?

Something To Think About:

A GAMBLER WINS AND NEVER QUITS, A WINNER WINS AND NEVER GIVES UP, SO WHICH ONE IS DESTINED TO LOSE?

Something To Think About:

WHAT IS A DREAM COME TRUE? SOMETHING THAT HAPPENS YOU NEVER DREAMED OF, OR SOMETHING YOU'VE DREAMED OF BUT NEVER THOUGHT COULD HAPPEN?

Something To Think About:

UGLY TRUTH OR PRETTY GOOD LIE, WHICH ONE LOOKS BETTER TO YOU

Thoughts Of Wisdom:

JUST BECAUSE SOMEONE SMILED AT YOU, DOESN'T MEAN YOU'RE NICE, JUST BECAUSE SOMEONE LIKES YOUR STYLE DOESN'T MEAN THEY ADMIRE YOU, IT JUST MEANS THEY'RE BLESSED

Thoughts Of Wisdom:

SURROUND YOURSELF WITH HAPPINESS AND YOU'LL LIVE A HAPPIER LIFE

Thoughts Of Wisdom:

A SPEECH IS POWERFUL IF SOMEONE WHO WASN'T THERE CAN QUOTE A LINE DECADES LATER

Thoughts Of Wisdom:

YOU'RE NOT CONSIDERED THE BEST UNTIL YOU BEAT THE BEST THAT EVER DONE IT

Something To Think About:

WHAT HURTS MORE THE TRUTH OR A LIE? I WOULD BE
LYING IF I TOLD YOU A LIE

Something To Think About:

A BEGGER IS NOT THE ONE WHO IS CONSIDERED GREEDY,
IT'S THE ONE WHO SAYS NO

Thoughts Of Wisdom:

HOLDING ON TO MEMORIES DOESN'T CHANGE THE WAY
THINGS REALLY ARE

Thoughts Of Wisdom:

LIFE IS TOO BIG TO LIVE SMALL

Something To Think About:

IS IT BETTER TO BE FULL OF BEAUTY OR BEAUTIFUL?

Something To Think About:

IS CHANGING OUR WAYS A SIGN OF BEING ASHAMED, OR WANTING TO GET BETTER?

Something To Think About:

WHEN DO WE REALIZE WE TRULY CARE FOR SOMEONE?
WHEN WE DO THINGS JUST TO PLEASE THEM, OR WHEN
THE THINGS WE DO FOR THEM PLEASES US?

Something To Think About:

THEY SAY MONEY MAKES THE WORLD GO AROUND,
BUT ONLY THE RICH GET TO GO AROUND A WORLD OF
MONEY

Something To Think About:

A PERSON WHO IS DEAF HAS AN EXCUSE THEY CAN ONLY HEAR THEMSELVES, BUT THEIRS NO EXCUSE FOR A PERSON WHO TALKS TOO MUCH AND NEVER LISTENS TO OTHERS.

Something To Think About:

DO WE CONSIDER OPENING UP TO SOMEONE SHARING OUR DEEPEST THOUGHTS WITH THEM, OR REVEALING THE FACT THAT WE REALLY DON'T LIKE THEM?

Thoughts Of Wisdom:

WHEN YOU BELIEVE YOUR OWN LIE THAT'S WHEN YOU'VE LOST TOUCH WITH REALITY, WHEN YOU CAN'T ACCEPT THE TRUTH, THAT'S WHEN YOU BEGIN LIVING A LIE.

Thoughts Of Wisdom:

IN LIFE YOU CAN HAVE SOME OF THE GREATEST EXPERIENCES BUT THE GREATEST EXPERIENCE OF ALL IS LIFE.

Thoughts Of Wisdom:

LIFE IS A GIFT FROM GOD, SO DID YOU EVER CONSIDER
GOD IS A GIFT IN YOUR LIFE

Thoughts Of Wisdom:

BE THE LEADER OF THE PACK, DON'T LET THE PACK LEAD YOU

Wisdom In The Quotes

You want to learn something won't you come inside
Because a teacher is not a teacher until they step aside
And the people with ideas, usually thinks about it
But it's the ones with the knowledge who did it, read about it.
They say the ones with talent got the ability
But it's the ones with the skills with versatility
The pursuit of anything is what you set
The reward of everything is what you get
God answers prayers so what have you prayed about
Ask him to give you something that you've dreamed about
They say the beauty's in the picture and the pictures out
So picture us trying to picture what you read about
Change the channels in your life like the television
Paint a picture of your future with your own vision
Be a leader and be praised generations after
The younger children needs a page in another chapter
So show your brilliance and come into the spotlight
Let the cameras take your picture to get the picture right
Remember brilliance is in the one who discovered you
Because if they know you're brilliant, then they're brilliant too
So as you read my quotes hopefully you will find a message
The wisdom comes as you experience life lessons

Dedicated to my nieces and nephews (The generation after)

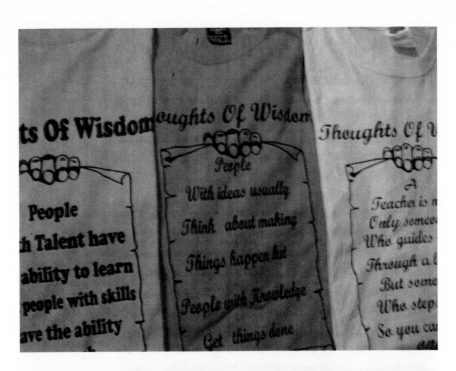

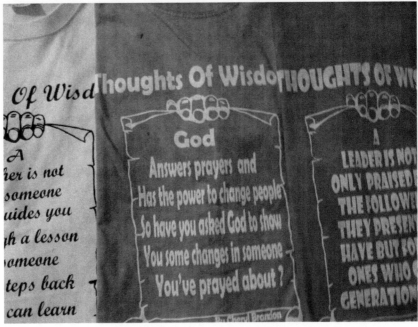

Wisdom In The Quotes

Listen

Hear when you listen
Listen when you hear
Don't just agree with me
And say yeah, yeah, yeah
Don't pretend my words
Are getting through to your ears
Because I can see right through you
When my words disappear
Don't get upset
And tell your friends that I'm nagging
Because you'll be upset
If I told you to start packing
So why can't we talk
Just too straightened things out
Because making things right
Is what listening about
So hear when you listen
Let's communicate with each other
Don't let it go in one ear
Just to come out the other
So listen to your woman
When she wants to talk
Because if she wants to talk
That means she's ready to walk
So listen up, listen up
Before you make me flip
And if you didn't hear that
Then read my lips

OFTEN MEN CALL IT NAGGING WHEN WOMEN WANT TO
TALK BUT WE'VE DISCOVERED ITS JUST MEN DON'T LIKE
TO LISTEN

Who Is This?

Who Is this?
Is this the one I know?
Who is this?
This can't be how we grow
Who is this?
I thought I knew you well
You say this is you
So be yourself so I can tell
This can't be how we laugh
It seems its how we cry
We can't get by on half
This can't be how we try
Who is this?
Seems I don't even know your name
But if this is you
Then you're the one to blame
So tell me, who are you?
This is what I need to know
And if you're not the one I knew
Then let your true colors show
So who is this? Who is this?
I'll ask you one more time
If this is the real you
Then you, could never be mine

God, Love And Me

He has my mind healing
He has my heart healing
He has my body repenting
He has my soul needing
Who is he? He is my God

He has my mind dreaming
He has my heart beating
He has my body shaking
He has my soul yearning
Who is he? He is my love

She has my mind wondering
She has my heart dancing
She has my body romancing
She has my soul sharing
Who is she? She is, no other than me

What Is A Union?

A union can be two people saying, " I do "
A union can also mean, I'm not doing extra work for you
A union means respect me then I'll respect you
A union also means yell at me I'm yelling back at you
So when I think of a union I think of unity
Not only in the workplace but in the community
A union is about the great stories we tell
Especially the ones that sends management to hell
And when I say hell, I mean winning a fight
While they're having trouble sleeping we're having a goodnight
So what is a union to you? , What is it to us all? ,
It has to be more than just the pictures on the wall
For me it's about the joys and pains we all share
Whether it's your story or my story we've all been there
A union can be something like a sport
But we'll only win with teamwork, then the balls in our court
So being in a union is not about becoming a star
It's about changing today for a better tomorrow
Now I could of wrote a poem about the trees and the flowers
But I'd rather talk about wages and hours
So when they pick a fight, I know I'm winning
Because a fight isn't a fight without union men and women

I wrote this poem at Cornell University in August 2004. I attended a summer course for women in the union. We had talent night and my former professor at Cornell Labor School asked me to participate because she remembered how I wrote quotes (UNION QUOTES) Example: Seniority means, Rice with Beans. I thought to myself what should I write about and I decided to write a union poem. I dedicated this poem to women organization STITCH, my former local 6 organizer Miriam Joffe-Block, Susan Tindall professor at Cornell Labor School, former co-workers at Holiday Inn Midtown who fought with me for our first contract, Freddie Jones formally of Laborers local 472 Pat Lamborn and Ellen Thompson in UNITEHERE recruitment, local 100 entire staff for giving me a union home, special thanks to ;
Jose Maldonado and Gilbert Palacios.
This is a movement

I Remember

I remember the days when I had to be in early
I remember when I use to wear my hair curly
Infact, I remember my mother with an Afro puff
I remember the days when parents didn't take any stuff
I remember the days when entertainment was at the Apollo
It's because I remember those days I think of tomorrow
I wonder where did our yesterdays go
And if we can see our future, we can see ourselves grow
I remember when kids loved going to school
And having house parties was considered cool
I remember when girls would play double dutch
And the clothes you wore to school didn't have to cost much
I remember all the girls loved to play hopscotch
And when the guys played basketball the girls would watch
I remember when people loved their neighborhood
And being friends with your neighbor was considered good
I remember when music was made for us to party
They say, today we make music to hurt somebody
What's going on, was a song we use to play
Now we got it going on, is the song we play today
I remember when respect was a given
Today we respect the dead, and disrespect the living
I wonder how did life get so re-arranged
I remember things clearly because clearly things changed
I don't like things now, that's why I think of then
Now and then I remember, I still remember when

Best Friend Gone

Here I go again, with my pad and pen
I dedicate this poem to my best friend
And anyone who lost someone they love
No one can replace someone you love
He passed away 4 years ago
I shed tears 4 years ago
4 months ago, 4 weeks ago
4 days ago, 4 hours ago
He said to me, Cheryl if I should go
Play a song for me, and make it slow
And when you play that song, make sure you sing along
And never question God because he's never wrong
Just pray for me, and hope he let's me in
And when you enter heavens gate, we'll be friends again
But until then you must live on
And treat life like your favorite song
Like Marvin Gaye, what's going on?
Heath Mills, I know your heart is torn
She would always say, " I was like your sister "
I was there with you so I know how much you miss her
I dedicate this line to your beloved mother
And just so you know, you truly are my brother
And to my cousin Nikki, I didn't forget you girl
Your father was the greatest uncle in the world
To my aunt Edna and my uncle Shine
I know your up in heaven, so you can help it shine
To Delores Boyd, who lost her only child
I wrote a thought for you I hope that makes you smile
To my niece Masa who lost her son
I know your hurting inside but there's another one
To my father he lost his first born
He may have passed away but now he's living on

To Mona Robinson who lost her little brother
Rus, Tito, Sharmaine, Darren lost their brother
They also lost their father my mother lost her brother
To my cousin Dez, we miss baby brother
Rhonda Jackson, I know you miss your mother
La Tanya Grier, I know you miss your mother
Trina Basey, I know you miss your mother
Tanya Hamiliton, I know you miss your mother
Jean Lauture, I know you miss your mother
Cathy Smith, I know you miss your mother
Camilla Woodley, I know you miss your father
John lost his mother, Darren lost his father
Jennifer Hudson, I know y'all miss your mother
I know your sister miss her son, I know y'all miss your brother
I can't imagine what you're going through
Soon as I saw the news wanted to write to you
So this is my verbal prayer for you
Many pray for you and your sister too
I can't forget Ms. Nicole Bell
Sometimes I try to forget, it's a cold world
He was too young to lose his life
You didn't get to say, " I Do " but you're still his wife
And their a reason I'm saying this song
Gerald and Sean Levert memory lives on
I still play his slow jams, on and on and on
But DJ don't play another love song
That's what he said in his last song
He was known and loved for his love songs
And to Eddie Levert, brother you stay strong
And I hope you like what I wrote in this song
So let us bow our heads and let us pray
And as my lyrics fade out let the music play
Because my best friend's gone

IN LOVING MEMORY OF EVERYONE WHO PASSED ON

Expectations

Look for me to do right but don't expect me to be perfect
Expect me to know right from wrong so you can understand I'm worth it
Look for me to share your dreams but don't expect me to give up mine
Expect me to be your dream come true so you can understand you are mine

Look for me to love you but don't expect me to ignore your flaws
Expect me to work on mine so you can look forward to changing yours
Look for me to stay home sometimes but don't expect me to be locked in
Expect me to make our house a home so we can look forward to staying in

Look for me to cherish our relationship but don't expect me to give up my friends Expect me to treat you like my best friend so you can understand what a best friend is

Look for me to be honest with you but don't expect me to tell you everything Expect for me to tell you what's important so you won't worry about the little things

Look for me to believe in God but don't expect me to be religious
Expect me to put God first and I hope God's first on your list
Look for us to be happy and we won't expect anything less
Except for us to be happy then we can expect happiness

Deep

Deep
Down Deep
As deep as I can go
I got down deep
Down deep in my soul
I got so deep
I couldn't let go
Now I'm so deep
Because I met my soul
We talked, we laughed
We prayed, we cried
I never knew I could get so deep
So deep inside
So when I looked
As I stepped outside of myself
I said, I had to dig deep
To get to know myself
Now I may be too deep
For someone else
And if you're as deep as me
Then introduce yourself

16 And 22

Carol wasn't one to play hookie
But she started staying home
So she could hang with Cookie
Cookie was one who never went to school
Never cared about books
So she chose to break the rules
Her parents never kept an eye on her
Cookie was the average girl hanging on the corner
But Carol thought she was fly I don't know why
She had a different name by every different guy
And I'm not talking about honey
More like tramp, slut or hoe
Because she would freak for money
Ain't a damn thing funny
When you're labeled as a freak
Turning tricks and giving up your treat
Well anyway Carol wanted to be her friend
And that's how the story begins
Carol was 16 and Cookie was 22
Carol said I'm old enough to hang
Can I be down with you?

16 and 22

Derrick was the average drug dealer
Slyest kid on the block
And he drives a four wheeler
And Sean wanted to be like him
Wanted to hang with them
So they made him the squealer
He had to watch out for the cops and crooks
They trusted little Sean so much
They let him keep the books
But Sean didn't know his debt
The books is where the truth comes out
And where the secrets were kept
And Sean wanted to get paid
He said 10 g's for the tapes and books
Let's make a trade
But now money is on his head
Another young brother shot
Another young brother dead
Sean was 16 and Derrick was 22
Sean said I'm old enough to hang
Can I be down with you?

16 and 22

Bill wasn't one to kiss and tell
But he bugged out the next day
When his private started to swell
Linda wasn't one to use protection
But she slept with him anyway
Knowing that she had an infection
Now Bill needs a doctor
His friends called him up for the news
He told them that he rocked her
But deep inside he was mad that he did it
But to his friends he won't admit it
Now he's known as a real Casanova he's a lover
Now he can hang with his brother
Bill was 16 and Linda was 22
Bill said I'm old enough to hang
Can I be down with you?

Life lessons are the best experiences and sometimes the best experiences are the lessons learned.

Yesterday And Today

Yesterday it was raining
Today it's sunny outside
Yesterday I walked with shame
Today I walk with pride
Yesterday I saw the city
Today I see the world
Yesterday I was just pretty
Today I'm a beautiful girl
Yesterday I wrote a verse
Today I wrote a song
Yesterday you came first
Today you tag along
Yesterday I asked the questions
Today I give advice
Yesterday was no exceptions
Today I think twice
Yesterday I was the audience
Today I draw a crowd
Yesterday I spoke with silence
Today I speak out loud
Yesterday we saw our fears
Today we see our power
Yesterday we had Bush
TODAY WE HAVE OBAMA

TODAY WE CAN BELIEVE IN CHANGE

C And C

Her name begins with a C
Some says she's full of herself
She said I don't need friends they need me
Some would say she's fooling herself

She has a twin sister
Her name also begins with C
She says I'm nothing like my sister
And my sister's nothing like me

C likes to brag and at times can be a bore
The other C likes to give credit because she is very sure
C has an ego that's big and no one wants to meet
But C ego's just fine and everyone falls to her feet

One of them is here tonight
So let me clear up your suspense
I always get mistaken for my sister
She's conceited I'm convinced

Who's That?

He passed by the sent of his cologne
Issey Miyake!
Who's that?

He walked by with her she used to be alone
Ugly Betty
Who's that?

She introduced me to him he smiled and shook my hand
Nice teeth
Who's that?

I'm seducing him in my mind last night I had a dream
Ooh Kevin
Who's that?

I woke up and there's a note left by my bed
From Kevin
Who's that?

My Performance

Put me on a stage
I'll perform
I'll play the character
That keeps you warm

My performance is my energy
My performance is my drive
My performance is that spark
That's keeps us alive

I'll always perform
When the audience is you
But I want you in this performance
Because only you know what we do

No one can play me
Just like no one can play you
So get ready to perform
Act one scene two

So when you put me on a stage
Perform with me
Because everyone wants a leading role
And when we do this next scene
Get warm with me
Because only you perform stunts in my soul

Graduation

Today is the day to wear that cap and gown
I'm graduating today this day has finally come around
I look up at my friends as no one makes a sound
The aisle seems too long as we start walking down
I'm trembling because this day has me nervous
But I feel good inside because I know I deserve this
After the long days and the late nights we studied
The only thing I'm sad about is I'm leaving some buddies
Also leaving great professor's who challenged me to get A's
And I challenged myself because education pays
So as I take the stage to receive my award
I heard my name called then I heard them applaud
Walked off the stage and I took a seat
Now it's back to the stage to get my degree
This is the main event time to take my hat off
And shout out to the world I knocked another goal off
And I'm not done because theirs another chapter
At the next graduation I'll be getting my master's

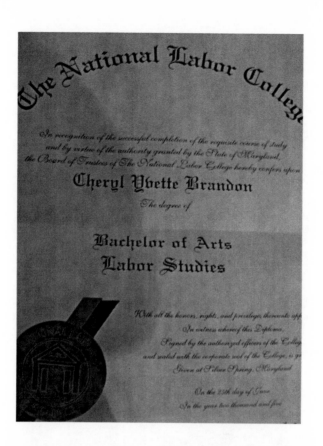

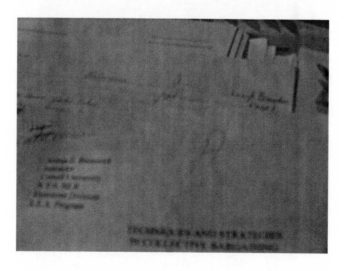

The New York State School of Industrial and Labor Relations
A Statutory College of the State University

at

Cornell University

This is to certify that

Cheryl Brandon

has successfully completed the course requirements of

The Labor Studies Advanced Certificate Program
conducted by the Metropolitan District Office in New York City

June 2005

UNIVERSITY OF BALTIMORE
School of Public Affairs
1304 St. Paul Street
Baltimore, Maryland 21202

MASTER OF PUBLIC ADMINISTRATION
PROGRAM

Hosted by

Mother's Day From Above

If today somehow seems to get you down
Think of all the people you still have around
Although our friendship may have changed its pace
When I think of someone special
I still see your face
You may have lost your mom
But you've gained another sister
My prayers go out to you
Because I know you truly miss her
I knew she liked me
Because of the friendship we have
She told jokes in front of me
And she made me laugh
So don't cry little sister
I know she's in a better place
She's probably dressed up today
In all white lace
So send her a kiss
And send her some love
Because she's wishing you
A Happy Mother's Day from above

Dedicated to Rhonda Jackson
In loving memory of Ms. Hazel Jackson

Reverend Richardson

Reverend Richardson was blessed
With a beautiful soul
She shared her life with God
Until she was 87 years old
When she spoke with God
She always spoke very loud
God knew she loved him
I know that made him proud
She was loved by her family
And admired by her peers
She always stood up for God
And rarely sat in any chairs
God wanted her to sing about him
So he gave her a voice
She sure could sing about him
Yes Lord, you made a good choice
Reverend Richardson
Was strong enough to raise 7 children alone
Although her husband passed away
She kept God in her home
When she went to Church
She would stay all day long
Every time she felted God's presence
She would sing another song
God said, sing one more song down here
And then you can take a bow
Because I'm taking you upstairs with me
To sing songs with angels now

In loving memory of Rev. Emily M Richardson

A Change In The Weather

The sun shines the wind blows the rain falls
I go through ups and downs when mother nature calls
Although I love the sunlight at times it's too bright
It takes away my vision and I can't see the light
The sun is not faithful because it comes and goes
And sometimes it will fool you and let the wind blow
The wind hangs out with the sun but it never stays the same
I grit my teeth at the wind, when it's mixed with the rain
The rain likes to tease sometimes with a few drops
But sometimes it pours down hard and never stops
When I'm out in the rain I get all soaked up
When I wake up to the rain I don't want to get up
When the weather changes I frown and I moan
I made it through the storm now the storms moved on
It's time to pack my bags and head out of town
Because winter is coming and the weather's changing now

Oh, That's God

It's quiet but the sounds of birds are in the air
No one is around but I know someone is here
The sky has a bright sun that is about to rise
As I watch the sunset I see beauty in front of my eyes

I'm searching for a rainbow red, yellow, green and blue
As I look up to sky I sense someone is watching too
Hello, hello is anyone out there?
Although I can't see you , I know you're standing right here

But the waterfalls answers me with a loud pour
You chose to give me a sign that's all I was waiting for
So as I stand in this water with my fishing rod
I heard sounds I thought I caught a fish
Oh, that's God

Price Tag

I came into the spotlight
Wearing a price tag
Money can't buy me love
But it can buy me the right to brag
They say money don't grow on trees
Therefore I've planted a garden
They say money is the root of evil
But I feel blessed when I'm shopping
Prada, Gucci, Channel, ah Louis Vuitton
I don't care what the price tag says
I'm buying those Christian Louboutin
Give me the Black Glama Mink
Because it's one of the best
I don't care what the price tag says
My answer is still yes
Give me that Cartier watch
In fact in his and hers
We don't have to discuss prices
I brought money out ready to splurge
I want that diamond bracelet
And the ring with the princess cuts
They say diamonds are a girl's best friend
And I love my diamonds very much
So if you want to send me on a vacation
You can send me to Hawaii
But I come wearing a price tag
Can you afford to buy me?

A Powerful Woman

Who makes us strong? Who makes us stronger?
Who keeps us standing, when we can't stand any longer?
Powerful women, that's who we strive to be
A powerful woman, who is she?
Who gives birth to a child, when a child is born?
Who gives life to a child and helps that child's life live on?
A powerful woman, I'm talking about a mother
A powerful woman, a woman you can't compare to another
Who is your first friend, you shared all your secrets with?
Who is, your best friend and truly your best gift
A powerful woman, I'm talking about a sister
A powerful woman, you must listen to her
Who is the one, who gives love from her heart?
Who is the woman that helps you finish, and helps you start?
A powerful woman, I'm talking about a wife
A powerful woman, a woman who can change your life
A powerful woman doesn't gives up when things get hard
A powerful woman is a woman who loves God
That powerful woman is also that career lady
That educated woman that sophisticated lady
But a powerful woman gets lots of knowledge from college
She also gets wisdom from life experiences and challenges
A powerful woman can wear many hats
As most women do, now how powerful is that?

Dedicated to mothers, sisters, wives, career women, teachers
Women are very strong and we have proven we are just as
Powerful as men

Hillary Clinton running for President is an example of
how powerful women can be

Dirty Mama

Sex and more sex
And when she's finished, she asks whose next
On her list, she'll grant your every wish
Come give dirty mama a kiss
Reminisce as you dig deep in her dish
Mama never said, they'll be days like this
A young daughter taking sexual orders
A nymphomaniac, but who taught her?
Was it you or her friends?
It doesn't matter because now she's driving a Benz
Her pockets are filled with twenties and tens
She gave up her skins
Now she's confessing her sins
Dirty Mama's on her job
She likes them big and chunky
You don't want to get involved with Dirty Mama
She's funky
Out for revenge she went on a binge
Had 5 to 10 guys and would say they were friends
The only question asked, was where's the cash?
Money can buy you love
But her love wouldn't last
Because soon she'll be loving another
She never told them she loved them
She was a money lover
And if your pockets weren't right
She'd say not tonight
You would have to show the green
To get the green light
Some people say, how could she choose this life?
And some would say money talks, so le's talk tonight
Dirty Mama's on her job
She likes them big and chunky
You don't want to get involved with Dirty Mama
She's funky

Special

You know you're special, special to me
You know you're special yeah ooh boy
I worship the ground that he walks on
I love it when he sings me a love song
He's every women dream but he's my desire
You know what I can feel the fire
That's burning I can smell the flame
I think of love every time I hear his name
Whispers in my ear so soft and clear
And make sure I hear every word your saying dear
Ooh my love you make me feel good
I will give you love like no other women could
They say love is blind but I can still see
How special he is to me
You know he opens the door when I'm coming in
And he pulls out my seat when I'm sitting down
You know that makes some girls just want to frown
But that only makes me want to hang around a little longer
And let the feelings grow stronger
My love was cold and you help it warmer
You touched my heart in a special way
I'm living proof that's it's safe to say
Ooh my love you make me feel good
I will give you love like no other woman could
They say love is blind but I can still see
How special he is to me
Can anyone understand what I'm going through?
If you have someone special to you
Believe in love with your heart and soul
Never leave your love out in the cold
Because as you grow old I was told
It's better to be warm than to be cold
And I hope by now my man can see
How special he is to me

I'm Only Human

Just because I forgot to say my prayers last night
Doesn't mean I don't believe in God I'm only human
Just because I pulled out a few hairs last night
Doesn't mean I have a bad temper I'm only human
Just because I didn't want to shake hands last night
Doesn't mean I'm not social I'm only human
Just because you wasn't in my plans last night
Doesn't mean I have fun without you I'm only human
Sometimes I will make mistakes but understand I'm only human
Sometimes I'll do what it takes so just appreciate what I'm doing
I'm only human so understand when I cry
It doesn't make me a weak person if tears fall from my eyes
I'm only human so yes sometimes I bend the truth
I would never want to hurt you if you can't handle the truth
I'm only human so excuse me if I pass you by
Does it mean I'm human if I believe I could fly
Just because I was a gifted child when I was young
Doesn't mean I knew I would share it with the world
It doesn't make me conceited if I'm convinced
It just means I'm a confident girl
I'm only human so yes sometimes I like to be praised
At times I read my poetry to myself and I am truly amazed
But I'll give God the credit, what I can do remains to be seen
Just know I'm only human, a gifted human being

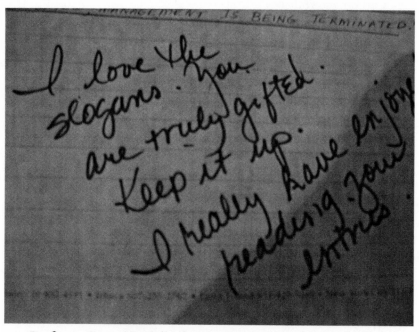

Professor Susan Tindall of Cornell Labor School wrote these comments to me. Notice she says I'm gifted LOL

In The Heat Of The Moment

Infatuated your love I'm waiting for
You got me screaming for more and more and more
Let's get cozy pour me a glass of wine
Come and hold me let me make you mine
I got something special you can bet that!
It's time to get sexual so lay back
Get a pillow lay your head on it
Let's get busy because I know how bad you want it
And if you feel a sensation, say ooh dear
I'm in your ear because your fingers are through my hair
The body movement is there so I'm convinced
I say ooh yeah to build up your confidence
You get so excited you begin to sweat
I'm getting wet because the mood is set
So it's time to explode
I hope you know body heat is the access code
So why don't you turn off the lights
So we can get into having us a good night
So I'll slip in a CD so we can grind
In the heat of the moment you're naturally mine
In the heat of the moment won't you satisfy me
In the heat of the moment baby try me

3 o'clock comes around
Were still going at it steady up and down
Your in a trance you can't even speak
It's safe to do my dance because baby I'm your freak
So put your mind in park and relax
Put your body in drive to reach your climax
Then say yes rest your head on my breast
Don't say nothing, I know it was the best
It felt good or should I say superb?
Shhh baby don't say a word
Let's just lay here and make some plans
The love was too deep for a one night stand
Do you agree? Yeah I thought so
You want to be with me because you just can't let go
It's the best you had in a lifetime
Don't confuse reality sex with a sex rhyme
I had you going you should feel ashamed
I want to know how many guys came
If you did only you would know it
You'll do anything in the heat of the moment
In the heat of the moment won't you satisfy me
In the heat of the moment baby try me

So if you want romance lend me your ear
I got you all excited I caught you out there
I'm just a romancer I like to get cozy
I'm the best private dancer somebody told me
I do my best dance under the covers
I know this song can relate to all the lovers
And if you feel that you have some sex appeal
Then baby, it's got to be real
So won't you focus on getting a partner
Girl don't squeeze his back unless you use some nail harder
And guys don't forget your safety kit
Because if you do, you know I ain't with it
Make sure you don't have many lovers
Cause you can catch a disease from many others
Practice safe sex or you might be next
On the terminator list with the x
So be careful just as long as you want it
Remember you'll do anything in the heat of the moment

Practice safe sex

The Birds and The Sky

Flying in the sky, group by group in a flock
The sound of birds in the air
That's what we call sweet music
The sun awakes and it's has it's place
The sky gets big enough to see it closer
From the joy of spring approaching
They dance and sing their songs
Together as they go in one direction
The sky changes colors as the day goes on
We look up to see the planes as they pass by
The good year blimp has a message written all over the sky
We love to see the rainbows to see the colors shine
We look up to the sky when something's on our mind
The fulfillment of togetherness as the day begins to erase
The sun starts to go down and the moon shows half its face
Now its time for the stars to take over the sky
Taking the place of the sun because they both love to shine
You can reach the sky if you believe there's magic in it
If you believe you can fly remember sky is the limit
So until tomorrow approaches and we can see the daylight
It's time for the sky to say goodnight

It's A Party

This is one of those retro songs
This is one of those let go songs
Party people throw your hands in the air
And just feel good songs
If you want the Champagne out
Or if you want to let the pain out
Listen to the melody of the song
And let the dam thing out
Music's here to make you feel good
Music's here to ease your mind
Remember back in the days when music played
We would form a soul train line
Now we got bump and grind
Now we got electric slide
We use to tell the people in the back
To wave they're hands from side to side
I'm here to make you dance
Here to make you clap
Here to reminisce
Here to take you back
We can go as far as you want to go
As long as we can play the track it's a party

It's a party y'all it's a party y'all won't you get up and party
It's a party y'all it's a party y'all won't you get up and party

Friday's Disco tunes
Sunday's Gospel tunes
But it was Saturday nights live at the house
R & B was in the living room
And if you want a slow jam out
If you want a Jazz tune out
We would play Miles Davis
Before the night was over
We'd bring Smokey out
Music's here to touch your heart
Music's here to touch your soul
Matter fact, my favorite song right now
Is Heaven Sent by Keyshia Cole
But I still love the old jams
Nothing's quite like the slow jams
We would put the Isley Brothers
In between the sheets
When the nights were cold
Music makes romance
Music made me rap
Here to reminisce
Here to take you back
We can go as far as you want to go
As long as we can play the track it's a party

It's a party y'all it's a party y'all wont you get up and party
It's a party y'all it's a party y'all won't you get up and party

Now that things have changed
But some things never change
And every time I heard Gerald Levert sing
I thought about the O' Jays
Then when R. Kelly came out
And brought Mr. Biggs back out
Imagine being at his concert
And seeing Mr. Biggs walk out
Mary J. Blige got soul
Patti and Aretha got soul
But don't think Whitney can't come back
She had a voice like gold
Soon as Barry White went out
Luther Vandross came out
And don't forget Michael hit us with a thriller
When Billie Jean came out
Janet made us dance
Prince made us clap
Here to reminisce
Here to take you back
We can go as far as you want to go
As long as we can play the track it's a party

It's a party y'all it's a party y'all wont you get up and party
It's a party y'all it's a party y'all wont you get up and party

Words

Words can be soft spoken like music playing
Words can touch your heart depending on who's saying
Words sometimes speaks louder than actions
With words sometimes you can get the greatest reactions

Words can make you feel better when something goes wrong
Words can be especially beautiful when expressed in a song
Words sometimes can brighten up your day
Words can express how you feel when you need something to say

Words sometimes can be the greatest thing you ever heard
Words touch us through God when you're spreading his word
Words are the best way to capture a heart
I love you is the best words you could say in the dark

I Need Love To Live

Knowing myself since I was a kid
I discovered I needed love to live
I met love when I met my Mom and Dad
When I came into this world it was something I had
Searching for love somewhat like theirs
I discovered I loved God by saying my prayers
Throughout my life I was a special child
Just knowing my sister loved me made me smile
Knowing I was loved also by my brothers
I felt I didn't need love from no other
But then I discovered that love never ends
Because I expressed love for my close friends
Love and I go together like a hand in a glove
On Valentine's Day I married the man I loved
Love can make you weak love can make you strong
I need love in my life to keep my heart warm
So love is something that I chose to give
Because I need love so I can live

Love

Your heart finally speaks when that feeling arrives
Your stomach sinks because you get choked up inside
Love is thoughtful, love is sharing, love is patience
Do you wake up with the one you love?
Or is the one you love, on your mind when you wake up?
Either way, this is a description of love
Love is encouragement, love is acknowledgement
Your compliments to each other can mean so much
Your hearts beats fast with the slightest touch
You think of your love as your day goes on
You and your love may have a special song
Or something in common that keeps you strong
Love gives you insight when something is wrong
Love doesn't come fast so it should last long
Love should be tender, soft and warm
No matter what, love should keep you truthful
Look at each other with love
And you will see love is beautiful
Love connects your mind, heart, body and soul
In the decisions you make love plays a role
Love is laughter, love is joy, love is supportive
Love is forgiveness, loves gives you strength
Love is a back rub, love is a walk in the park
Love is praying together at night in the dark
Love is respect, love is admiration
When things get tough it's that important conversation
Love is apologizing when you know you're wrong
And even when you're right don't argue long
Love, love, love what does it mean?
If you truly love someone
You will relate to these things

Alone

As she stands by her window longing for her someone
Wondering if he'll ever come back
She asks, what made him leave this way?
She interrogates her own mind asking herself why
And each time her answer is the same
She suffers from loneliness
So the thought of being alone intimidates her
He hasn't been around in years
But she continues to stand by her window
At times, she speaks to God
But never long because she's afraid of his word
She doesn't trust his word alone
Because she doesn't understand the meaning of it
This woman is alone but she still waits for him
Although he's never home, she puts out plates for him
Her children stares at her because they're confused
She doesn't explain why, she's singing the blues
She thinks she's alone but her kids are her company
And she leaves them alone so she can be free
Her Pastor once told her, she should move on
Because she's loving a man, that's already gone
If she stands by that window she will always be alone
But if she leaves that house she will find a new home
So put your trust in God and the word you once believed
And leave that house so you can finally breathe

Life is too short to be unhappy

I Seen It From My Window

I'm looking out my window at 4 o'clock because I was bored
I just came home from school and I had to do my chores
I couldn't go outside and play with the average kids
My father didn't like what the average kids did
And as I watched the little girls play double dutch
I heard get your hands up, it's another drug bust
People started running, some was even on the ground
With their hands behind theirs backs and they still beat them down
I seen it from my window, what's going on?
This is how it is when your living in the ghetto
Pop, pop, pop I heard shots at 2 O'clock
I jumped out my bed to see who they got
Was it just another brother laying in the gutter
Not this time it was somebody's mother
And now her poor daughter has to make it on her own
It's bad enough they were all alone
It's a damn shame that she had to leave this earth
Just because she wouldn't give up her purse
I seen it from my window, what's going on?
This is how it is when your living in the ghetto

Back in my window it must have been half past eight
And here's Karen escorted home by her date
He didn't walk her inside, gave her a kiss and said goodbye
She said thanks the dinner was great
Now here comes these three guys with a shotgun
Looking for someone to get and they got one
Karen tried to run but she couldn't escape
The next thing you knew the poor girl was getting raped
Right outside and people were passing by
And didn't lift a finger to help when they heard her cry
It wasn't their business they don't want to get in this
Because cops don't give protection when it comes to a witness
So they just walk on by like they don't see
And I get out my window so they won't see me

It's a crying shame it has to be like that
Will things change? You can forget that
I seen it from my window, what's going on?
This is how it is when your living in the ghetto

Glad I'm in my window therefore no one can bother me
Because every 20 seconds around my block there's a robbery
I'm hearing, give me all your jewelry and make it fast
And while you're at it give up your cash
There's always something going on in the streets
That's why I'm in my window when I supposed to be sleep
Just the other day a young boy committed suicide
Jumped off the roof he thought he could fly
No doubt in my mind he was high
I wasn't there when he cried for help but I seen him die
It makes me want to shed a tear that he died like that
But face reality he must have been on crack
There's nothing you can do about it, what can you say?
That's just the problems of the world today
And I've seen all of this on the down low
Being nosy looking out my window
I seen it from my window, what's going on?
This is how it is when your living in the ghetto

INSPIRED BY TRUE EVENTS

The Perfect Match

He is her music
She is that special song
For her it took a long time
For him it didn't take long at all
He is her ray of sunshine
She is the sunshine of his life
He is her new world
She is the beginning of his new life
He is her sense of humor
She is his joy and laughter
For her, he is that good book
For him, she's that final chapter
He is her dream come true
She is the answers to his prayers
She is his tears of joy
He takes away all her tears
He is her strength
She helps to keep him strong
For her there's no suspense
For him, he knows when something's wrong
He is her future
She is his days to come
For him, she is his one and only
For her he's the only one
She likes it when it's sunny outside
He likes it when it rains
For him she is that fire burning
For her he's that burning flame
He is the love letters
She is the poetry in motion
She is that river flowing
He is that wave in the ocean
For him she comes first
For her no one is above him
He is the one who knows what love is
And she is the one who loves him

The Blues For A Union

Woke up this Morning with a lot on my mind
It's another day on the strike line
Woke up this Morning turned on the news
Until I get affordable health care I'll sing the blues
I've been on this job since 1995
With these raises I'm getting I won't survive
And my boss keeps yelling at me
I want a union for respect and dignity
Woke up this Morning at half past ten
I going down to my job but I'm not going in
Woke up this Morning took me a shower
We'll show our boss today who's got the power
When we stand united the company will see
They shouldn't mess with our schedules or our seniority
They make us work for free I'd rather pay union Dues
So until I get a fair contract I'll sing the blues
Woke up this Morning to a rainy day
I want to stay home but I want better pay
Woke up this Morning ready to fight
If it means I'll get a Pension I'll fight all night
And I can't afford to buy a new pair of shoes
So until I get an increase in wages I'll sing the blues

ARAMARK STRIKE VICTORY!
Historic gains for NYC cafeteria workers in three-month strike.

On November 12, 80 Aramark workers at New York Life and 55 Water Street in New York City went on strike to win new contracts. In December, Aramark's ...gant – as if the workers would not last another week. ...ave in. The workers stood strong and

Hooked

It wasn't me that had you hooked it was the drugs
I found out too late that drugs is stronger than love
You made a commitment to finish what you start
Your commitment to drugs is what broke my heart
I thought that our love would keep you on a high
But you got high off the drugs and kept flying by
I finally realized you didn't love yourself
You admitted to drugs you didn't love on one else
How could you be so faithful to something so bad
It made you feel good but it made you look bad
It made you throw away everything that we had
But deep down we had nothing drugs looks at me and laugh
So it's time I forgive you for what you put me through
You're hooked on drugs and drugs are hooked on you
So as I live my life I'll continue to pray
And maybe you'll ask God for your life back some day

Strive For More

Everything I have
I'll strive for more
What I got today
I'll strive for more
What I want tomorrow
Makes me strive for more
Give me a little more
And I'll strive for more
Take it all away
I'll strive for more
No matter what they say
I'll strive for more
On any given day
I'll strive for more
Day after day
I'll strive for more
Ask God when you pray
To help you strive for more
Like you never did before
You must strive for more
When you can't go no more
You must strive for more
If they won't open up some doors
You must strive for more
Even if you're sure
You must strive for more
Anything you want in life
You must strive for more
Because life gives rewards
When you strive for more

This Is Who I Am

I swear to tell the truth and the whole truth
Let me stop right there I don't owe the world the whole truth
Only God knows who I am and God only knows the plans
He gave me some gifts that I chose to share with you
This is who I am, am I somewhat like you
At times I'm very quiet because I like to observe
At times I'm very loud when I'm speaking my words
This is who I am, a Tom Boy who loves basketball
If there was a game to win yes I tried to win them all
I was an honor student throughout most of my years
Respected by most, admired by most of my peers
I was a favorite but I treated others the same
To protect someone else sometimes I'd take the blame
I was kind of rough and yes I knew how to fight
I kicked a few butts but it never felt right
I'd prefer to be friendly and treat people good
But if I had to get mean believe me I would
This is who I was when I was young
This is who I am now, am I the chosen one?
Still very serious but now I have lots of laughs
A sense of humor is a gift we should feel blessed to have
I know life is too short to choose the wrong path
I still go to the movies with my mom and dad
This is who I am and they didn't do bad
I believe that family should be your comfort zone
This is who I am, but sometimes I enjoy being alone
This is who I am I married the one that I loved
I would do it again because I believe in love
This is who I am I love playing with kids
I didn't have one so it's important I give
God said give something back as long as we live
This is who I am so this is what I chose to give

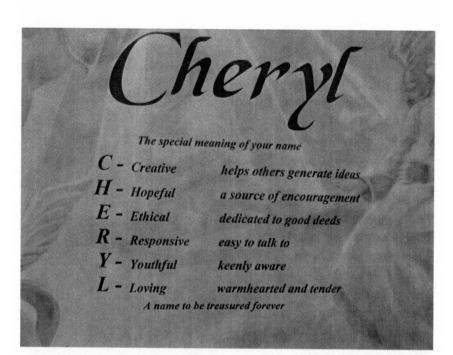

Cheryl

The special meaning of your name

C - Creative   helps others generate ideas
H - Hopeful   a source of encouragement
E - Ethical   dedicated to good deeds
R - Responsive   easy to talk to
Y - Youthful   keenly aware
L - Loving   warmhearted and tender

A name to be treasured forever

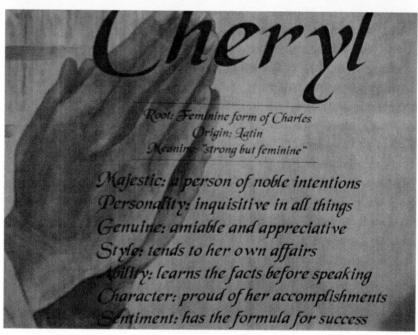

Cheryl

Root: Feminine form of Charles
Origin: Latin
Meaning: "strong but feminine"

Majestic: a person of noble intentions
Personality: inquisitive in all things
Genuine: amiable and appreciative
Style: tends to her own affairs
Ability: learns the facts before speaking
Character: proud of her accomplishments
Sentiment: has the formula for success

This Is Who I Am..

My Sister

I dedicate this poem to my little Sis
Sis I know I've never told you this
But I admirer you
Although you admirer me
You've become a complete woman
And I'm still working on me
You've done some things
I'm still looking to do
Even though I say you're bossy
I love the mother in you
You give me energy
To do the things I do
You've shared your life with me
And I'll give my life for you
You are my best friend
And I love you the most
There's nothing like a best friend
That's why I'm keeping you close
Sometimes we may argue or disagree
I still value your opinion
Because you're important to me
At times I need your advice
Although I'm older
You can lean on me
But at times I need your shoulder
So as we live our lives
And look forward to days to come
You say I am yours
But you are my number one

Love you sis

Me and my Sister

A Mother

Once upon a time God created a mother
Who nourished and comforted you like no other
She told bedtime stories while you were under the covers
A woman who gave you a sister or brother
A mother is the first one to show you true love
God assigns her as your protector from up above
She brings you here to help guide you through life
A mother's love is needed for the rest of your life
A mother is your teacher away from school
She gives you guidance to follow her rules
She sacrifices her life to make yours good
She'll be there for you when no one else would
And as you get older she becomes that best friend
A friend that comes once in a lifetime and never again
And as a parent she'll always hold her spot
And tell you the truth whether you like it or not
At times she may need a help and hand
You'll do anything for her because you're her biggest fan
And even when you think you know it all
When your looking for answers it's your mother you call
So if your mother is alive give her some praise
Tell her you love her and respect her ways
And if she passed on let her know you miss her
And tell her you love her and blow a kiss up to her
A mother's love can never be replaced
Because when I think of my first love I see my mother's face

DEDICATED TO MY MOM

The Future

Yesterday was history
Tomorrow is unknown
The future is a mystery
Knock, knock whose home?
No one knows what lies ahead
Time just keeps on running
Nothing can stop the future
Because the future keeps on coming
Some may be nervous by what they don't know
Because the future has a face that never shows
Some may be excited because they like to be surprised
Although the future has a face, it wears a disguise
So prepare for the future
Because we can't change the past
Your future is coming and it's coming real fast
And even when we prepare
The future changes plans
Tomorrow is just a day away
But tomorrow is in God's hands
The past, the present, the future
In that order is how we say
The past is gone, the present is now
And the future is on its way

26 On Black

You stay up all night
Rolling the dice
You won the first time
But now you lost twice
You're thinking to yourself
You can beat the odds
I'll win this next hand
Because I'm good at cards
All bet's on the table
So you better think fast
26 on black
Now I'm losing more cash
I know I shouldn't again
But 26 on black
Yes, yes I won again!
That's how they reel you back
Until I win big I'll keep on going
You're blowing on the dice
But its money you're blowing
I can't leave now
I have to win my 3 g's back
26 on black, 26 on black
And the winning number is 12 red
So I tried my last hand
On 12 red instead
I'm leaving this table broke
I heard screams so I looked back
The dealer said the winner is…
26 on black

Life is a gamble but never gamble with your life

Protect Yourself

Take 10 people worried about their health
And 9 out of 10 of them, is not protecting themselves
So you figure 9 people are out there spreading the wealth
But it's that 1 selfish person who seems to love their self
A sign said do not enter and everyone clearly saw it
So you decided to protect yourself and everyone else ignored it
But who are these 9 people, does this sound like you?
Maybe not this time but it can happen to you too
Now we got 9 people in the waiting room awaiting their fate
The Doctor comes out with bad news to speak with 1 through 8
As you're counting your blessings, you hear voices in your mind
It's Mr. HIV waiting to speak to number 9

Hi my name is AIDS, how did I skip you?
You didn't use protection I can't believe I bypassed you
Well I'll get you next time because I know you like to charm them
You don't think I exist because you never use a condom
But I'll get another chance because you don't care about your health
I'll just wait in someone else body because you don't protect yourself

HIV/ AIDS IS DESTROYING OUR YOUTH, PLEASE USE
PROTECTION!

Cold

Shivering, shaking with her hands fold
The weather's not the reason this woman's so cold
As you hear her voice her bitterness unfolds
Now the ice has broken right into her soul
This woman's been hurt maybe once or twice
If you want to get to know her you must break the ice
When she enters a room its about 20 below
Because she's holding on to her pain and she can't let go
And even when the sun shines she's blowing smoke
A woman becomes cold when her heart is broke
It's going to take time for some warmth to be felt
Because she's a snowman with no intensions to melt
So the next time you see her shivering and shaking
Just know that she's cold because her heart is aching

She Said No

He came in one night and he closed the door
She said please stop I can't take this no more
She tried to scream but he covered her mouth
She begged and she pleaded for him to get out
He hit her and shoved her as he ripped off her clothes
She's being raped and abused but nobody knows
He's her mother's boyfriend so she feels ashamed
And somehow believes that she's the blame
How could her mother love someone like this?
He takes her body but from mom all he takes is a kiss
How can she stop him she wants to escape!
Although she says no she's still being raped
She has nowhere to go and no one else to talk too
He said if you tell someone no one would believe you
She asks why does her life have to be so sad?
She finally asked her mom where was her dad
Her mother confessed she was a victim of abuse
She said your father raped me that's, how I got pregnant with you

If you are or ever been abused please talk to someone they can
Help, and don't ever think it's your fault because it's not.

Recognize

Recognize your spiritual side or whatever it is you believe in
I saw some miracles happen so I recognize how much I need him
Recognize your husband or wife or the one you share your life with
I recognize that I've met someone who I believe is truly gifted
Recognize your kids when they do right but teach them right from wrong
Can you recognize a good kid when you see one if you don't have kids of
You're own?

Recognize your mother and father or the one who raised you as a kid
If you feel they guided you through life recognize everything they did
Recognize your sister or brother but what if you're an only child
How will you learn to care? Will you recognize sharing how?

Recognize that special teacher or the one who mentored you
I recognize I had some good teachers but it's life that really teaches you
Recognize a true friend when you meet one because they are hard to find
You will recognize a real friend when you meet one because they are
One of a kind

Recognize someone's achievements especially if you didn't receive
I know we can be anything we want to be I recognize we must believe
Recognize a strong woman recognize a strong man
Recognize Obama and Michele and recognize YES WE CAN

Black Coffee

Do you like your coffee with cream?
Or do you like it black?
If I can't smell the coffee beans
You can take it back
I need some strong coffee
To get me through the day
So bring me some black coffee
So I could stay awake
Sometimes I like Hazelnut
Sometimes I'll take it light
But black coffee has an effect
That keeps me going all night
Just the smell of those beans
Sneaking up my nose
Black coffee keeps me warm
When the wind blows
It's sort of an addition
It's sort of a fix
You can take it straight up
It doesn't have to be mixed
This coffee's so strong
You might not know what you're feeling
If you have too much of it
It will have you hitting the ceiling
You can get black coffee
At many different places
This particular coffee
Has been in many different faces
And even though you've been around
I'm dedicated to you
I can't give up my black coffee
I'm addicted to you

This Picture

Look at this picture
And tell me what you see
This picture's not perfect
But it's beautiful to me
The size is just right
And the colors are bright
It can be a beautiful picture
If you see it in the light
Now look at this picture
And tell me what needs to change
This picture is lonely
It's clear this picture needs a frame
To give it some life
So it will never fall
Every picture needs a place
Up on a wall
Now here is a picture
Clearly with no flaws
I bet that's not its true picture
Behind closed doors
And if only someone
Could be a fly on the wall
You will see that picture's
Not perfect at all
One picture says this
The other picture says that
One's a motion picture
Because it's all an act
So picture someone
Painting a picture of you
Now look at this picture
And see if it's you

No School On Sunday

Monday through Friday we all go to school
But school on Sunday wasn't a part of the rules
We had English class, Science and Math
We told our teachers we knew our history
And all they did was laugh
They told us about Harriet Tubman
Because they wanted us to know we were slaves
But Jesus Christ died for our sins
Because he wanted our souls to be saved
Did you ever go to school on Sunday?
Did you ever hear the choir sing?
Do you know as much about God?
As you know about Martin Luther King
Saturday night we went out and danced
Sunday mornings we skipped class
Were starting to get better grades in history
But Sunday school we never pass
So who teaches class on Sunday?
Let's go to Bible school
Because until you go to class on Sunday
You haven't really finished school

What Kind Of Job Is This?

Step up step up your hired on the spot
This is a shitty job and it doesn't pay a lot
A union can make it better
Without one you're fired on the spot
What kind of job is this?
Is this the job you've got?
When it comes to health insurance
You can't afford to pay it
The company's plan cost too much
And the boss doesn't want to pay it
Last year you didn't get a raise
This year they gave you 15 cents
This year they also cut your hours
So really you didn't receive a cent
What kind of job is this?
A union can make it better
Let's gather all the pissed off workers
And let's fight the boss together
We can make this a better place to work
If you just add your name to the list
No one should receive a 15 cents raise
What kind of job is this?

Dear Lover

I'm writing you this letter
To let you know I have no regrets
In case I've never told you
You're someone I'll never forget
Dear lover...
Do you remember the day we met?
Do you remember the walk in the rain?
The day we both got wet
Do you remember the white castles?
We used to eat late at night
I know you can't forget
Those playful pillow fights
Dear lover...
Writing you seems kind of strange
Especially because I know
Both our lives have changed
An even though we both
Have the same last name
I wish we could go back to being lovers
When it was fun and games
So dear lover...
I hope this brings back memories
I know you can't forget
Those special deliveries
I know you didn't forget
Those red satin sheets
I know you still enjoy
The chocolate covered treats
But most of all I know you miss
When it was just me and you
Can we go back to being lovers?
I miss the satin sheets too
I'm writing you this letter
To let you know there'll never be another
I want to go back to fun and games
What happened to my dear lover?

No Lady In This Bed

Put me in the kitchen
And I'll cook up a good meal
String beans, rice, potatoes and veal
I'll even run your bath water
So you can relax in the tub
I'll massage your shoulders
And give you a back rub
When you're in the living room
I'll have your slippers on the floor
I'll treat you like a king
Who could ask for more?
Around our family and friends
I'll always be polite
I'm a lady in the day
But someone different at night
So meet me in the bedroom
I'll make you blast off
The masquerades in our bedroom
It's time to take this mask off
I don't mind talking dirty
Because I've always been a lady
But when it comes to the bedroom
Hell, I've never been sweet Sadie
But there are some secrets
That a lady must keep inside
Only the one you love
Should see that bad girl side
When were dining outside
You can bet I know how to act
But when it's a king size bed
You better watch your back
I'll bring you your paper
Even greet you with a smile
But being a lady in bed
Is just not my style

So you don't have to worry
I read what the sign said
It said, DO NOT ENTER
If a lady's coming to bed

My Calendar

January is the month I was born
So I love January for that Birthday song
February is the month I discovered love
I love Valentine's Day for those chocolate doves
March is the month that ends all the cold weather
I love marshmallows in March by the fireplace together
April is the month my sister was born
Everybody loves springtime because winter is gone
May is the month my younger brother was born
Memorial Day cookouts, burgers, chicken and corn
June is the month everyone's out of school
I love the first day of summer I love jumping in the pool
July is the month to see the lights in the sky
Star's can be beautiful but nothing's like the Fourth of July
August is the month my older brother was born
But I get a little sad in August because summer's almost gone
September is special because it's my mother's birthday
But I'll never forget the 9/ 11 when the world trade center went away
October is the month my father was born
And he's the one who loves to sing those birthday songs
November is the month we get together and eat
I give thanks in November for our family retreat
December is the month we create our shopping list
I love December because of the bright lights on Christmas
We have 12 months, 365 days in the year
But again January is my favorite month
Because I look forward to see another new year

Heart Attack

I sneak up, beating real fast
Pounding and pounding
To see how long you can last
Get you sort of in a chokehold
Until you can't breathe no more
You may not know how to handle me
Because you've never met me before
Somebody should have told you
Your heart's not protected
Sometimes I'll give a warning
But most times I show up unexpected
So if you know someone whose met me
And they are still alive
Congratulations they must of beat me
But the odds are still 1 out of 5

Mr California

When I first met you
I wanted you to be mine
Mr. California...
You brought me sunshine
You brought me beautiful weather
When the sun wouldn't shine
Now I'm dreaming of California
All of the time
I grew up in New York
But it's time for a change
Because all New York brings
Is cold weather and rain
California has beautiful trees
And a very bright sun
Mr. California...
I believe you are the one
I'll always love New York
Yes this is true
But that California weather
Has me wanting you
Not only for the weather
But you've made my heart warmer
I love New York
But I'm in love with California
So Mr. California...
I have one question for you
Will you be my sunshine?
Because New York and I are through

And God Said The Devil Is A Liar

And God said let there be light
Is that why we turn each other on?
And God said we must have faith
Is that why all our hope is gone?
And God said believe in me
Is that why the devil taunts us with temptation?
And God said send your prayers up to me
Is that why the devil wants us to believe he doesn't listen?
And God said live a life of holiness
Is that why the devil wants us to be sinners?
And God said love thy neighbor
Is that why the devil wants us with no friends?
God is a true God the devil is a liar
So don't believe anything the devil says
And God said, he'll take you higher

A Girl's Best Friend

I love the way she shines
She is one of my best friends
Although she has other close friends
She'll be with me to the end
I know she represents love
Because the one I love gave her to me
I've loved her before I loved him
But he brought her back to me
Some of her family lives with me
But I chose to keep them in a box
Because she is the one who is close to me
She never hides under the rocks
When I look at her sometimes I get hypnotized
She looks so crystal clear
I can see my face in her eyes
Whenever I go out that's when I go out with her
That's when she likes to shine
She knows no one can compete with her
Sometimes she changes colors
Sometimes she changes her name
Princess cut or baguette
I love her just the same
And even though she'll have you broke
She continues to make me spend
I won't leave home without her
Diamonds are a girl's best friends

Beating Like Drums

Boom, boom, boom
Beating like drums
Lumps all over her face
As big as plums
He puts the keys in the door
And she hates when he comes
Who would ever think!
She'd hate the sound of drums
In pain, she yells and screams
Hoping someone would come
But no one heard her scream
And she's too afraid to run
Boom, boom, boom
The beatings begin
He's beating her like drums
Over and over again
He left her on the floor
To hear the sounds of her cries
She crawled up in the corner
With tears in her eyes
She's angry now
With revenge on her mind
She said, this man has beat me
For the very last time
She stood by the door
Waiting for him to come
He walked in, she slit his throat
Now she doesn't have to run
She held a kitchen knife
As if it was a gun
Her hands still shaking
And now her hearts
Beating like a drum

When Cops Are Around

Do you feel safe, or do you fear for your lives?
When cops are around
Because now they're known as bad guys
The boys in blue are wearing a disguise
With a license to kill and they're taking lives
But what about the cop that does his job right?
He's behind his desk doing paperwork
Each and every night
Lets re-evaluate the officers were giving a badge
Because a lot of these officers are giving us body bags
I may not know the statistics on murder and crime
But if cops are becoming murderers
How can they stop crime?
So when cops around do you feel safe?
Is it safe to say, some cops need to be replaced?
I want a cop around, who wants to serve and protect
No one wants a cop who likes to serve with his teck
So the next time I hear shots
I want the cops to come running
I don't want to run from the cops
Because I hear shots coming

Ms America

Ms America
You thought the world would be true to you
Especially because we sung
America the beautiful
You thought the American people
Would love you and only you
We left, but now were back
Because you made us believe in you
You told us we'll be heard
And you didn't let us down
You finally let us speak
That's why were back in town
We knew Ms America
Wouldn't let this country drown
Although the waters were deep
We still kept swimming around
You showed me I could survive
When you gave me a lifeboat
You kept our dreams alive
And told us to get out and vote
So Ms America, Ms America
You made our dreams come true
And I'm one of millions of people
Who still believes in you!

Dedicated to the United States of America

A Black Man's House

Congratulations, we finally got a win
George Jefferson was moving on up
But this time were moving in
No more neighborhood watch
And petitions to keep us out
This time all of the decisions
Will be made in a black man's house
So it's time to remove
Those old writings on the wall
And let's put up some pictures
That can relate to us all
As we walk through this white house
You'll see a black man in the hall
You'll see a black man in the room
You'll see a black man on the wall
And at the head of the table
This black man will be waited on
This is now a black man's house
That all White House is gone

Dedicated to President Obama

You

Instantly when we met
Something made us connect
I felt a feeling of warmth in my soul
You made my smile resurface
Very honest and direct
That warmth I felt went from head to toe

You opened my eyes
Now I close my eyes when I think of you
My heart's been waiting at your door
You made love to my mind
That's why I dream of you
And now my body's coming back for more

You love God and you shared it
You told me to pray
I was lost
But you helped me find my way
And nothing can compare to this
It's a reason you're here
I thank God for you each and everyday

An Angel Came Around

Her water broke
And her bundle of joy arrived
He wasn't on schedule
And he brought someone with him
He came early to be a surprise
He saw some light
Met his mom
And left his brother here on earth
He said hello
But he was in a rush
He wanted to get to heaven first
An angel came around
But God has him now
He's in his crib in heaven
Laughing and playing around
Although she met him briefly
She wanted him all to herself
God said since you have two angels
I'm keeping one for myself

In loving memory of Rhanel Louis Francis

Like Pearls

Beautiful like snowballs
Like marbles when they swirl
Like diamonds when they shine
I love you like pearls

Like Easter Sunday
Like flowers when they bloom
Like a 50th anniversary
Like the first night on a honeymoon

Like a beautiful morning
I love you like Christmas Day
Like the stars that shine at night
Like Spring in the month of May

I love you like blue water
Like crystals you can see clear
Like the colors in a rainbow
I love you like fresh air

But I love you like pearls
Because you're a precious jewel
You remind me of pearls
Because pearls are precious like you

I Can't Believe You're Gone

As I look at your pictures
I still can't believe you're gone
At times I shed tears
When I hear your favorite song
La, la, la, la, la, means I love you
I'm reaching my arms out
Wishing I could hug you
I'm trying not to cry
And believe me it's hard
But when I cry, its tears of joy
Because I know you're with God
Does he like the way you cook?
Does he like the music you play?
I still can't believe you're gone
I think of you everyday
When the sun shines
I look up to the sky and smile
When the rain pours
I think, what is she doing right now?
And if there was a way
I could turn this world around
I know you like it up there in Heaven
But I'll ask God to send you back down
So while you're up there pray for me
Because it's hard to carry on
It's so hard to say goodbye
I still can't believe you're gone

Dedicated to Heath Mills
In Loving Memory of Earlene Mills

Purify Me

Bathe me, purify my soul
Take me down in the waters
That feels so cold

Speak to my mind, cleanse my body
Touch my heart, renew my soul
Make sure when I leave here
I have a better place to go

Although I want to be here
Only God knows my fate
Purify my soul ole lord
I want to get through Heaven's Gate

So bathe me in these waters
Free my soul from all my sins
When I lay back in these waters
I want to rise up....
And begin again

A Quarter

Can you spear a quarter?
I'm homeless
I really need a dollar
But I'll ask someone else for the rest

I figure if I remain silent
He may think I'm deaf
But I respond
I spent all my money
I don't have anything left

I'm lying...
Because theirs twenty dollars
In my pocket on the left
But do I have the right to remain silent
Should I ignore him because he's homeless?

Why do we ignore the homeless?
Why can't we help them buy a bottle of water?
Although I had 20 dollars in my pocket
I wouldn't even give up a quarter

I know he didn't believe me
He looked like he didn't want to ask
I didn't care that this man may have needed me
I ignored him because he needed a bath

Can you spear a quarter?
He asked the next person as he walked away
You would think he asked for a million dollars
Because everyone turned and looked away

So I said, Mister before I give a quarter
Theirs something I must do today
I said, here's my last twenty dollars
For every quarter that I've turned you away

A Pocket Full Of Curses

Mr. Pissed Off (seeking help)

Shit, damn, what the hell is going on?
This shit's been happening all week
Turn my fucking lights back on
I had a hard day at work
So please leave me alone
My damn cable got cut off
So did my fucking phone
Shit, these bills are killing me
What the hell am I going to do?
Why is this shit happening to me?
Does this shit ever happen to you?
I need another job
Better yet, I need to find a partner
What the hell is going on?
This shit is getting harder and harder
I don't want to rob and steal
But damn, I'm running out of luck
I can't tell this shit to my landlord
Because he don't give a fuck

Hello Mr. Pissed Off
I'm gonna keep it real with you
With a pocket full of curses
No wonder shit's happening to you

Jail

I'm caged in
Locked in this 4 by 4 cell
It's no guarantee I'll make it to Heaven
But I sure made it here to hell
I know what you're thinking
My punishment should fit the crime
But do you think selling drugs
Should get me a whole lot of time
I know you say it's still a crime
And selling drugs is against the law
But my cellmate only got 5 years
And he blew someone's brains to the floor
How does the law work?
Is it designed for us to fail?
I've been doing a lot of thinking
I have nothing but time in jail
This cage is for an animal
And even animals need to be free
I wouldn't wish this life on no one
Oh lord, have mercy on me
The hours go by slowly
The days and nights takes too long
In jail, all you see is the same sex
So why is all this sex going on?
It's not safe here
In fact, it's worse than being on the streets
I saw some cruel things happen here
Inmates being raped and beat
They say jail supposed to be a place
Where felons come to get rehabilitated
But I say, jail is just a place
To come back and get reacquainted

Mr. and Mrs. Verbal Abuse

His
You'll never amount to nothing
Look at you
You're destined to fail
You've gained a lot of weight
You're not attractive anymore
And you don't even do your nails
I don't know what I saw in you
I've been living in hell
That's why I never stay home
And I want someone else
I should've married Michelle
You always complain to your family
Talking about all the things I don't do
Matter of fact
Get out my face
I'm tired of looking at you

Hers
Look who's talking
You can't keep a job
And a woman like me
You don't deserve
You never clean behind yourself
Talking about I'm not attractive
You fat slob, you got a lot of nerve
All my friends say I should leave you
I can do bad all by myself
And I don't want to either
That's why…
I'm sleeping with someone else
Matter of fact
You can pack your bags
This marriage has run its course
I don't have to take this verbal abuse anymore
I'm filing for a divorce

Darlin Dear: A Tribute To The King

What an inspiration
A young singing sensation
Your music's touched our hearts
Generation after generation
We grew up on ABC
I Want You Back
And I'll Be There
But one of my favorite Jackson songs
Happens to be Darlin Dear
And when your songs
Came on at the parties
Everyone would get up and Jam
There will never be another
Michael Jackson
You were a Bad, Bad man
That makes me think of
Who's Lovin You
Now that you're no longer here
Your music will live on forever
So that means
You'll always be there
Although we'll Never Say Goodbye
When it's our time we all will go
I guess we'll have to wait
Until we get to Heaven
To see you put on your next show
But in the meantime I'll reminisce
And watch you perform on the big screen
No one entertained us like you
You were a true Dancing Machine

Your moves were Off The Wall
And every move I tried to do
I never Stopped Until I Got Enough
In fact, I wanted to Rock With You
But I couldn't keep up on the dance floor
As I watched you on the television screen
I believe God brought you here
To make people all over the world Scream
No one can deny
You were the best that ever touched a mic
But it's time for you to rest now
You've been working hard all of your life
You gave us Thriller, Beat It
And my favorite was Billie Jean
You showed us it was Human Nature
And encouraged us to follow our dreams
So thank you for all the music
And the charities you gave to Heal The World
I never believed that you could hurt anyone
Let alone a boy or girl
And something tells me you're at peace now
As I write this, I'm listening to your song
So the Man In The Mirror can sleep now
Darling Dear…
Your legacy will live on

Dedicated to The Jackson Family

The Exit

I'm driving in this car trying to reach my destination
When I get to my exit I'll end this conversation
Seems as if I've been on this road before
I'm on exit 22 getting off at exit 4
There's lots of traffic so it may take me some time
I'm approaching exit 20 with a lot on my mind
Hoping these cars get out my way so I can pick up some speed
I'm driving on a full tank so I have all the gas I need
As I started driving down this road called life
I got off at exit 16 because I wanted to write
I wish to be a poet I want to be heard
I want to change lives with my spoken word
So I wrote a few poems at the rest stop
Now I'm back on the road exit 13 is the next stop
As I pick up some speed I want to go faster
I'm chasing a dream because it's my dream that I'm after
I'm doing 90 but I hope I don't get stopped
By exit 10 I'm reciting Hip Hop
So now I'm driving this car in another lane
Before I reach exit 8 I want people to know my name
So I started performing so I could get my name out
And as I performed, more people came out
I feel like I'm about to get my name in the mix
Started at exit 22 now I'm at exit 6
On the Apollo stage a star was born
I performed on that same stage where the legends performed
I'm starting to feel this dream is alive
I performed on MTV before I got to exit 5
My dream is coming true I'm almost at my destination
Before I could get to exit 4 I heard license and registration

Printed in the United States
222235BV00001B/3/P